MW00476263

WHY WOMEN PULL AWAY

A Cure For Relationship Frustration; Five Masculine Behaviors The Feminine Wants Forever

SEVA KENN

Editor: Nick May, TypeRight Editing
Cover design: 100covers

ISBN: 978-1-7336770-3-5

First edition

CONTENTS

INTRODUCTION

Your wife or girlfriend used to be so cute. She smiled adoringly. She was soft and feminine.

But now she has an edge. She's confrontational, distant, and brittle.

What's wrong with her? You think to yourself.

She used to compliment me. Now she mostly complains.

She used to want sex all the time. Now I have to convince her.

If you're in this pickle, you're not alone. Diminishing female enthusiasm is the norm. Through my unique lens as a sexual healer to over two hundred female clients, I will explain why enthusiasm wanes and how to get it back.

If you study this short book, you can achieve relationship parity with your female partner—at least, if she's not a narcissist (five percent of women according to the National Institute of Mental Health), primarily focused on career goals, or traumatized by abuse.

Fortunately, that still leaves about eighty percent of women, by my estimate, who have a prominent feminine side that longs for healthy masculine input. If that feminine side meets hostility instead, it slinks away to heal from the wounding.

PAIN AND CONFUSION

I'm a dude. I know how painful it is when a woman dials down her sweet sexiness. It doesn't make sense. You try to get back what you had during the good times. You put out a valiant effort. But every attempt to fix problems makes them worse.

Failure in front of your woman is the worst sensation ever. No amount of muscle or fitness can stop the steady uptick of cortisol that shrinks your ball sack and lowers your sexual allure. Your reproductive fitness is threatened.

The situation is maddening enough that some men resort to violence. If that worked—if that brought women back to a sweet and loving state—then a book like this would not be required.

But it doesn't bring women back. It pushes them further away. Women don't respect violence. They fear violence and respect competency.

But you don't know which specific competency. It's as if you're in a fight, blindfolded, with your hands tied behind your back.

A FALL FROM GRACE

Being in love put you on top of the world. You became addicted to that high, but now it's gone. No dealer on the planet can supply a substitute drug.

Nothing can replace that look of openness and giving in her eyes. You had no power to resist it. Then she took it away.

It's a terrible situation, but she is not purposefully trying to mess you up. She's just as messed up as you. The chemicals of infatuation that drove her all over you slowly dissipated.

That means, for the first time, you have to truly win her.

You may not like to hear that. It may seem redundant or difficult. But don't worry. Winning her is in your genes. If you find the groove, little effort is needed.

Until then, it's rejection and failure. You're a failure when you get defensive, insecure, and afraid or disguise those responses as judgment, sarcasm, and criticism.

You may believe yourself civilized and well-behaved. But you are not. You can't conceal your annoyances and displeasures. All she has to do is look at your face.

Your woman sees it all. She's sensitive to your body language, tone of voice, and word choice. She does her best to not be affected, but she is.

She'll shyly turn her head away or look down. You sense something has come between you. As the stress hormone cortisol replaces bountiful testosterone, your body knows you've lost a round in the sexual-competition ring.

NATURE'S PRACTICAL JOKE

It is, without doubt, a sexual competition. Until you are dead. You will never go wrong if you keep your primal, animal nature in mind.

To ensure reproduction, nature tricked your woman into falling in love with you. An excess of dopamine, a positive-reinforcement neurotransmitter, created a fantasy version of you in her brain.

It was fun and easy at first. Everything you talked about was a turn on. You wanted to have sex all the time. You were happy.

But after a few months or years, things changed. It became harder and harder to understand each other and know how to make things light, sexy, and fun.

That's when nature laughed uproariously about the practical joke it pulled. That is when a woman's neurotransmitters shift from pleasing to testing. Without the dopamine veil, she can see what's wrong with you and no longer treats you as perfect.

This is the way humans evolved, so we're stuck with it.

EVERYONE LOSES

An unavoidable truth: You will lose the woman you fell in love with.

That is at least the norm. You swept her away. Then she woke up and wondered what happened. It's heartbreaking for her too. She wanted to keep the thrill.

Falling in love was not under your control, or hers. It's a special treat, ravenously eaten until only the crumbs remain. That's when a relationship actually begins.

The in-love version of your woman is like a free trial. It's designed to get you hooked. But when the free trial ends, the monthly payments begin. Did your woman set up this clever scheme to unlawfully charge your account?

No, she did not. Mother nature set it up, and both of you are the marks. Rage against the machine of nature, if you like. But raging to get your woman back in line will fail. She may have fully committed to a relationship, but it's counter-productive to rely on that. It only highlights the weakness of your position.

So, is it hopeless?

Nope.

MEN ARE LIKE LIONS

Both of you are coming down from the in-love high. It's just as hard for her as it is for you, so your job is to help with that, instead of making it worse.

She stopped *automatically* loving you—stopped automatically wanting sex and laughing at your jokes. Accept that reality.

Through no fault of her own, her brain chemistry changed. She reverted to her normal state, before she fell in love. She has less motivation to give more than she gets.

Yet men, like lions, continue to lie around waiting for their mates to kill prey and bring them the delicious bloody carcasses.

Women emphasize their kitty side in the beginning. They can't stop themselves. They shower us with purrs, but when they stop, we growl at them.

BAIT AND SWITCH

We're victims of bait and switch, and we have to accept the con. Like the loss of our five-year-old innocence, the con is baked into life.

When our women change their view of our value, we have to take it with grace until we discover our masculine role.

Maybe you have a good job or business to bring to the table. That never hurts, but no matter how hard you bust your ass to make it, providing material comfort is not enough.

A woman's heart is the final arbiter of value. She is the judge. Look closely and you can observe her score card.

Her tells are there, because she's sensitive to the real or underlying meaning of everything. This is why she takes things the "wrong" way.

Your woman doesn't laugh when you fail to connect with her. It's difficult for her when you say or do the exact thing that brings her down.

This male-female disconnect is the norm. I've never seen a man that did not aggravate his woman. As ill-equipped for a sexual relationship as you may be, to your woman, ignorance is not a pass.

If you get angry when you don't understand, you hurt her. If you reject her vulnerable shares, you hurt her.

She shouldn't be so sensitive! You might be thinking. *She has no reason to be hurt!*

She will see such responses as a failed test by another typical male. There's nothing political or feminist about her grading. It's strictly personal.

HOW DO I KNOW?

During the years 2010 to 2013, my professional title was Sexual Healer. Marvin Gaye released his song *Sexual Healing* back in 1982, and Sexological Bodywork became legal in California in 2003, but sexual healing sessions were still virtually unknown to the public in 2010.

Clients found me through a retreat center specializing in tantra, the ancient art of sacred sexuality. The website listed me as a practitioner. Individual sessions lasted two to three hours, starting with dialog and progressing to touch, designed to soothe imbedded sexual trauma or reinvigorate lagging sexual interest.

My typical client was a forty-five-year-old heterosexual female, discouraged by a loveless, sexless marriage. She described herself as "broken," but it took only fifteen minutes of enlightened sensual touch for her to rediscover her sexual fire.

Based on research detailed in *What Do Women Want?* by Daniel Bergner, my clients' session experiences should be expected. A woman's native hotness is never dead. It's just been crushed.

Clinical test subjects in Daniel's book reported that exposure to a male stranger they found attractive restored their sexual appetite. Mere exposure was the surest way to achieve that restoration.

The women were not frigid. They grew cold because their partners iced them.

I don't believe men purposefully do that, but men's limitations become an impediment. All the times a man hesitates, resists, and gets defensive, add up.

The feminine has a diverse range of interests and a need for variety in all aspects of life, including sex. She wants to live life to the fullest. She wants to tango.

THE SEROTONIN FACTOR

There's a scientific explanation for this normal female behavior: Women's brains produce thirty-three percent less of the neurotransmitter serotonin than men's brains do. One effect of serotonin is a contented state.

Men's brains generously offer the state of contentment, but women have to work for it through their activities, pleasures, and emotional connections.

It makes sense, therefore, that women are more into yoga, massage, cooking, decorating, gardening, socializing, and aromatherapy. In these ways, and countless others, they use their senses to activate serotonin.

Many men believe their women should be as content or relaxed as they are and resent her need for the extra steps, or the extra effort, required for her to feel complete or satisfied.

But that resentment will never be helpful, because a woman's brain doesn't re-wire from negative pressure. No couple wins a protracted battle against female nature, so do the opposite.

Embrace female nature and collect substantial rewards, such as greater productivity, better sex, and deeper connection.

Lower serotonin production is also correlated with a higher propensity for depression and sensitivity to stress. Try to take in the power you have to destroy your partner through rejection, disgust, or passive-aggressive neglect.

Looking at it objectively, female nature does what it can to take care of the female it lives in. That should be encouraged. It lowers the need for male responsibility.

THE TEST BEGINS...NOW!

Your woman will express a desire, show an interest, make a request, or reveal a need that you weren't expecting.

"Let's learn tango!" she exclaims.

How swiftly can you up-level? This is a chance to heroically meet her needs without having to think. Just by saying yes. But her tango exclamation reminds you of stumbling around, awkwardly mis-stepping at your last dance lesson.

It only takes a second for her to see that you're not enthusiastic about her proposal. She sighs. Another potential joy bubble bursts.

Every day, your woman offers opportunities for you to be interactive with her. Self-centered fears or insecurities short-circuit them.

Women speak, emote, and dance as a way of living, not analyzing. Men can have trouble keeping up. There's too much data to process sequentially. When an enthusiastic response to "Let's learn tango!" doesn't come, the dead air is heavy.

Some experts in the relationships field will say that your woman has tested you, as all women will. Is it a test? Or just a woman being herself?

Women are less narrowly focused than men, can multitask, change subjects quickly, and burst forth with girlish delight. They would like it if you could keep up. They want a consort, not a computer.

If it's a test, you pass or fail within the first second. Every failed test leads to a harder one down the road until she reaches a conclusion about you.

Given the difficulty of passing tests, when a woman requests a service that her man can provide, he should welcome it. With gratitude.

That signals to her, in her language, that he cares. Such moments can convince her she is safe enough to express herself, at dinner, on the dance floor, or in the bedroom.

If you stumble over her tests, then you haven't got her. You force her to hold back. It will feel like she pulled away.

SHE LONGS TO FEEL FEMININE

Your male body and masculine character make her feel feminine, but so does getting stuff done.

What could be easier than taking out the garbage? Just do it. Wanting you to take out the garbage is not rational. She just likes to be helped. It gives her a feminine sensation.

Remember this formula: You are helpful = she feels feminine = you feel masculine. It's a win-win. You win if she feels feminine around you. She doesn't want help with everything, but she does when she asks. Jump on it!

When things get dicey, she will attempt to make it work. She will try to involve you, but you may view this move as aggressive, annoying, or interfering.

She pushes you by striving for what she wants. It's not strategic or tactical. She doesn't consciously think, *OK, now I'm going to test him by suggesting tango lessons.*

It's not planned, but the push is real.

Yet, too often, her partner puts up a deflector shield. He rejects her version of life. She then feels less safe and hesitates to be sexual.

NOTHING'S WRONG

It's not a matter of right or wrong. Both partners suffer through the post-in-love crash. But women attempt to understand what's happening.

However, probing makes most men grumpy. They're not in the mood for it, don't like it, or get stressed by it. These reactions speak loudly. They confirm her unease. She pulls away.

Women are not in control of their pushing, testing, and probing behaviors. They simply feel an emotional pressure and seek to release it. The pressure is nature, forcing them to decide if their man is a worthy mate.

TESTING BEHAVIOR

Men turn sour at the first hint of testing behavior. Underneath, women are attempting to get their needs met. The kicker is, most women don't fully understand what their needs are. So they try shit.

They feel an urge to say or do something, then they say it or do it. Spontaneity serves three purposes: personal expression, learning about themselves, and engaging their mates. Women are "live" all the time, instead of writing a script in advance.

Imagine your woman's face lighting up as she blurts out, "Let's go to Cancun for Valentine's Day!"

What is your first reaction? Does your face light up too? Do you have visions of sunsets, beaches, and romantic dinners? Or do you frown at the thought of paying for a flight and hotel?

Whether or not a trip is actually booked, your reaction to her enthusiasm is the crucial point. She wants to verify if you embrace life, or keep living at bay.

If she, or both of you together, can figure out how to vacation within your budget and time constraints, great. The habitual "no" limits her resourcefulness for you both.

The feminine needs fun, excitement, variety, and something to anticipate. Anticipation turns her on. It's suicide to tamp it down.

Women want to feel and do. Everything. They don't get everything, of course, but men often wilt from the constant pressure. Stressing about women's needs does not help them. Helping them get their needs met helps them.

HER PRIMARY NEEDS

Connection, love, and sex are a woman's primary needs. Meet those simple needs and all others become less important. As you shall see, her primary needs are the easiest to meet.

I assume that you and your lover at least desire sex. You may feel inadequate, but no matter how deficient you are, she chose you. But she has additional needs that determine whether she keeps choosing you.

Testing is a gentle first nudge. It can be so subtle that neither of you realize it's happening. Like a double-blind scientific experiment, neither the subject nor the experimenter knows the test variable.

This is how her subconscious wants it to go: in-love, test, get needs met, melt, in-love continues. But these are the actual results: in-love, test, failure, pull away.

From your perspective, she pulled away. From her perspective, you pushed her away.

You pushed away some part of her you didn't like. You don't get to choose specific parts of her. It's all or nothing. After the in-love phase, a man's limitations become visible, yet men expect female blindness to continue.

Make no mistake, women *want* to be soft and feminine, but their men don't know how to soften them. Men respond to testing with outrage. Outrage is a whine. Whining is decidedly not sexy to women.

Women itch for a man who can fully receive their ecstatic or tearful expressions until they peak and collapse. The more a woman expresses, the more fulfilled she is and the deeper she can relax into softness.

However well put-together a woman appears, she has a shy girl buried underneath. She may not tell you, but her girl needs care. It usually gets stomped on instead.

IT'S NOT ABOUT YOU

Women offer the gift of themselves to be cherished. But that's not what happens, right?

When:	Then:
She's excited about an idea	You trash it
She complains	You get defensive
She wants to do things	You drag your feet
She wants more from you	You feel pressured
She gets upset	You recoil
She wants clear signs	You express doubt
She wants your enthusiasm	You're depressed
She wants you to improve	You think you're fine
She resists having sex	You feel rejected

In every example above, you make it about you. Your reactions reject her. You do the opposite of what she needs. You force her to scale back.

Women are bubbly and happy, but you pop the bubble. Your default habits are powerful dampeners. Get out of your head and into her energy.

That means encouraging her to be herself and delighting in the result. So she can be mercurial, fanciful and expressive. Without a match from you, her fire cools.

Your woman can't implant what she needs into you. With all the pressures women face, not to mention their own journey of womanhood, the last thing they want to do is help their man be a man.

Do that by yourself, or with the help of a coach.

ENCOURAGEMENT IS UNIVERSAL

The human need for positive reinforcement is absolute.

Original research published in American Behavioral Scientist in 2004 and summarized in the Harvard Business Review concluded that participants in the most successful business teams used a six to one positive to negative input ratio.

Since sexual egos are particularly sensitive, the ratio may be even double for lovers. That makes a twelve to one ratio of appreciation to feedback. That is the baseline to keep in mind.

Appreciating your woman is a win-win. It gives her what she needs and takes you out of the thought realm, where your pain exists. Thoughts are more likely to be crap than gold, anyway.

Partner-critical or self-critical thoughts keep you separate, out of flow. It's easy to tell if you are flowing (empathetic) or not. Your lover's enthusiasm increases or decreases. Your opinion is useless.

She determines whether or not you are connecting.

With patience and discipline, go all in on her, giving her space to fully be. Flow with her high before you put in your two cents. Strategically, that gives you more time to upgrade your responses.

LET GO OF RESENTMENT

Every woman attempts to get her needs met. In principle, one has to accept things that can't be changed. Conclusion: Don't resent her for trying to get her needs met!

I get it. There are a million reasons to resent women. It can seem like a power imbalance that women control what goes into their pussies, and when.

But whatever your "reason" for resentment, it's not logical. Resentment is emotional. Specifically, resentment is a byproduct of your unique set of emotional triggers.

In my experience, the real resentment is toward oneself, for not taking effective action when stressful situations come up. Resentment toward women is misplaced. Women did not create the universe. They are just as subject to the biochemistry of love and sex as you are.

At first, an abundance of dopamine rendered you incapable of resentment. When your sensitive self returns, it feels like your lover is not as nice.

FLEXION POINT

The impulse to resent your lover is a flexion point. Out of habit, you may snap at her, thus communicating that you blame her for your discomfort.

But blame simply makes your lover defensive. Look at discomfort as an opportunity for growth. Your partner continually gives you chances. It's a good thing she does. Otherwise, you would both cruise along until one day she just disappeared.

Her tests are the greatest gifts to you she has. Through those gifts, you have the chance to become a better man.

Rejecting, resenting, or resisting your woman creates stress for you both. It's like being stuck in first gear on a downhill slope. Both of you feel the drag.

THE PAIN OF REJECTION

The eye candy of female beauty is everywhere, but it's mostly look-don't-touch, resulting in a conscious or suppressed feeling of rejection.

I believe the pain of rejection underpins men's resistance to embracing women's needs. The reward for effort—sex—isn't there. It's a primitive point of view, but useful.

Complaining about unrequited love does not help. The INCEL (involuntary celibacy) movement has proven that. The demand that women submit, even legislating that demand, is going nowhere.

An easy cure for rejection is to have fulfilling relationships with women. Join them rather than beat them.

Whether or not you are in a relationship, cultivating your positive qualities and abilities is the only direction that gets you closer to sexual and emotional satisfaction.

I encourage men to recalculate their fulfillment equations. Add in terms of pleasure and bliss that are always accessible within. As long as you're alive, your nerves are working. The opportunity to tap in to a sensation flow is always present.

Activating pleasant sensations helps to mitigate self-defeating thoughts and enables your body to radiate aliveness. Women are attracted to that aliveness.

A change in attitude or ability comes first, before relationship quality can improve. Find joy within yourself and through interaction with your lover.

I tell clients to "always be seducing." As world-famous relationship expert Esther Perel says, "Foreplay begins approximately after the last orgasm."

That's ridiculous! You might be thinking. *I could never do that. I could never be in the mood that much.*

Those reactions are examples of male resistance, resentment, and limitation that women find so frustrating. The "foreplay begins" idea represents the physical and emotional connection that women long for. It symbolizes possibilities instead of limitations.

Your mindset can change from *Fuck that!* to *Hmmmm, I wonder what that would be like?* It's a gear you can shift into when you are with her.

Here is a powerful abundance perspective: *I have so much love and sexuality inside of me, I can never exhaust the ways in which I play with it.*

I'm not advocating a life of sacrifice. Only an expansion of perspective in the feminine direction. Women want every moment of time with a lover to be enjoyable, not a constant manipulation to get penis into vagina.

It doesn't hurt to find the pleasure in every moment of intimacy and sexual innuendo. Such a tantra-like expansion of time and perspective improves your life and, ironically, your chances for great sex.

Seeing oneself operate in abundance takes away the pain of lack. Banish lack. It turns women off. Let in the possibility of variety and new experiences, when limitations threaten to bring you down.

WOMEN WON'T CHANGE TO SUIT YOU

Women's needs will not change. And they shouldn't, since they're inextricably linked to the continuation

of the human species. That trumps all other con-
cerns.

Something magical happens if you embrace needs
instead of hating them. Every need that you address
makes you feel more manly. There's no substitute
for that feeling. No amount of side-stepping does
the trick.

You get a testosterone rush when you turn and face
her. Like jumping off a cliff, do it without thinking.
Then you're in free fall, but will splash into the pool
of interaction.

The hard part is over. Relax and connect.

You may think you are in over your head. That you
will run out of air and die. But that's inaccurate. You
are simply feeling emotions that have stopped your
breathing.

So breathe and survive. It's okay if you struggle. It's
obvious to her anyway, so hiding it gets you nowhere. She prefers that you struggle with something
instead of denying it. She respects you for trying.

You don't have to be perfect. No one is. But she
wants you to be your best in every way. Maybe you
cling to the freedom to be a bum. No one has the
right to stop you.

You can be as free as you want, but so can she. She can dump you. If you flatly reject any input from her, you shoot yourself in the foot. Basically, every reaction she has to you contains valuable information.

She wants you to pay attention. To focus on the intimate details. I get it. This is foreign territory for most men. We put up barriers to learning from females, but our brains get a rush from overcoming our own resistance.

We try to avoid situations that highlight our lack of skill. That habit must be turned on its head. The Huberman Lab at Stanford School of Medicine has shown that failure frustration leads to the most efficient learning.

I recently used failure frustration to dramatically improve my frisbee forehand throw. Ultimate frisbee is one of my joys in life, but I criticize myself after a game.

For ten years, I suppressed these thoughts, while my forehand remained weak. But shortly after viewing sucky throws as a gift of information, I began experimenting.

I tweaked my body position, arm angle, wrist angle, grip, and follow through. I had no idea so many adjustments were possible until I allowed myself to examine my failures.

TRIGGERS SUCK

Frustration, anxiety, and overwhelm can strike at any moment during an interaction with your lover. It's easy to conclude that she caused your downturn in mood.

She will feel your prickles. As much as you believe your thoughts are private until you make them official, you announce them through facial expression, tone of voice, body language, and word choice.

You're upset, but your woman is not the reason. Realistically, nobody "causes" it. Triggering happens too fast for it to be intentional. It always catches us unprepared.

You will be triggered and overwhelmed. You'll feel hopeless and incompetent. That sucks, but the sooner you manage the situation, the sooner you'll return to the life you prefer.

For an in-depth discussion of trigger management, see chapter six in my book, *When Lovers Attack: How to Stop Fighting and Get Back to Sex.*

SHE DOES NOT CONTROL ME!

As knowledgeable as I am, I still get triggered.

On a recent Saturday, I was scrolling the news in post-breakfast drowsiness, enjoying some needed relaxation. That's when my partner, Cheryl, walked in and announced she was going to Home Depot to buy some new plants for the backyard.

Then she added that I should dig holes for the plants when she returned. Digging holes in the scorching sun was not in my plan for the day.

I felt a rush of indignation. She put a plan for me in motion, without my consent.

In my younger days, I would have made Cheryl's offense against my autonomy the issue. *She doesn't control me!* I would have thought.

But I've learned what an energy suck that is. It's female nature to include partners in what they do. And, most of the time, they want to do something useful. It's a bad idea to stop them.

"Offended" hormones surged through my body for a second before my brain came up with an antidote: *Cheryl is putting out the effort to drive to another town, browse the options, and pay for her choices. I don't like those activities, but I do like digging holes. That circulates my blood and boosts my test-osterone.*

Then I get to enjoy the beauty of the plants when I see them in the garden. That's a long-lasting benefit for only twenty minutes of effort. I would not choose to get more plants. Cheryl saved me energy by not asking my opinion about it. I'm glad she took the initiative.

That antidote worked. It saved me a bout of snappishness and the extended aftermath of cortisol-fueled negative thoughts toward Cheryl, and later, myself.

CAVEMAN REACTIONS

Your lover will expose your tantrum self, also known as your privileged male ego. Caveman reactions might release pent-up anger, but they offer a very poor cost/benefit ratio.

No doubt you're familiar with the costs. Several days of tension, uncertainty, and impotence, while self-critical and partner-critical thoughts proliferate.

What is a successful course of action? Try this exper-iment: The next time you have the urge to snap at your partner, stop and feel the sensations of that urge. Note how your body feels.

Then approach her and tell her how exceptional she is for a specific reason. Feel the sensations of appreciation inside of you. Observe her pleasant surprise.

Compare the before and after conditions.

I have learned that my caveman reactions don't serve me. They keep me from exercising parts of myself I don't volunteer to exercise.

My female partner brings me something that I need, if I can let it in. She desires better living for us both. I am often more strictly self-centered than that.

KEEP UP WITH THE CHANGES

Women may, overall, have more needs than men. Reproductive organs and hormones significantly complicate a woman's biology, like they are more than just one human.

Consider yourself lucky that women take responsibility for their biological imperatives. It forces them to be more demanding than they're encouraged to be.

The upside is that their needs give men an opportunity to be masculine. Women give back by expressing more appreciation than a man might expect.

When you first met, or when you fell in love, you effortlessly met her needs. But then her needs changed. They became more real, more concrete.

Let go of the past in order to keep up. That will allow you to focus on fulfilling her needs in the most efficient manner and with the least delay.

The more you resist, the harder it becomes. She will not give up, ever. She will manifest either her happiness or her sadness. There's no in between. It's your choice which one.

The pressure she puts on you is good for you, if you let it in. She pushes you toward your most creative, potent, and developed self.

You probably need pushing. Thank her for that and rise to the occasion instead of throwing a tantrum. It is most efficient, most rewarding, and least painful to skip ahead to meeting the need. As in, right now!

ALARM BELLS

At this point, alarm bells may go off in your head.

Isn't what you're describing enabling? Wouldn't meeting my woman's needs make her weaker and more dependent?

In a word, no. Being a baby makes her weaker. Overriding her, criticizing her, overlooking her, minimizing her, and deflecting her needs weakens her.

If you disparage a woman's needs, to satisfy your sense of fairness or alleviate your fear of manipulation, you cut off your future with her.

You may feel she has too many needs. That is inaccurate.

What she has too many of is *attempts* to get her needs met. Since you rebuff those attempts, they recur frequently. What you're really afraid of is the feeling of impotency after you deflect her needs.

There's a simple solution to this fear. Meet her needs. Test it out. Start by paying close attention to her, delighting in what she says, and helping her when she asks. See what happens.

In my personal experience, and from observing clients, a woman's needs do not increase from being met. Meeting her needs satisfies her hunger.

The more quickly and completely you meet her needs, the more she can relax into her feminine self. Trust her to make that transition.

Her feminine needs attention, support, and empathy. It takes more energy to answer the demands of your ego, than to welcome her feminine. That gives her pleasure and she gives you credit.

IT'S NOT ALTRUISM

Helping her get her needs met is not altruism. It's a job, but comes with important benefits. For one, it gives you purpose.

Secondarily, she smiles, glows, and looks at you with gratitude. The value of that look is incalculable.

A relationship can be sustainable. Do a little and get a lot. Why resist the little? How hard is it to dig a hole or give her attention? It's only as hard as you make it.

You were not properly trained for relationships with women, but nobody cares about your suffering, right? I care very much, however. It hurts me to see men struggling so much.

The Buddhist philosophy of *all suffering is caused by attachment* has helped me a lot.

Eliminate suffering by accepting the reality of female nature, rather than fighting a war against it. Not only can you never win that war, but fighting female nature increases its destructive power.

RETRAIN FIRST IMPULSES

It takes practice to relax in the face of female needs. To be successful, retrain your first impulse. You will not be in the mood. It will seem too hard. It will seem like she doesn't deserve it.

That is your signal. That is when you activate a productive response, without knowing what you will do or say. The first step is breaking the fucking inertia.

Like putting on running shoes when you don't feel like running, you overcome a mental block, then circulation takes over and you run farther than you thought possible.

Overcoming resistance to the feminine is the same discipline. I learned that if I'm not in the mood for conversation, yet let myself get into it, my lover actually boosts my mood. That is my new normal.

MOOD IS CHANGEABLE

When I believed my mood was sacred, I resisted my lover's natural bounciness. Her aliveness, in fact, made me angry. I resented her for it.

My words and behaviors passive-aggressively sought to bring her down to my level. Mostly, I succeeded. That didn't bring me joy, however—only a moment of deflected attention. So I did not have to engage.

A normal woman will look to you for interaction and connection, more times than not. The pressure is on. A female life is before you. It is impossible for you to duck your role.

Don't resent the pressure. Think in terms of love and connection. That is a path of handling yourself. The real fight is with yourself. You defeat yourself when you get annoyed with your partner. Self-defeat is the actual enemy.

You are always leading yourself and your partner up or down, forward or back. You may think your woman is leading. She is not. She is expressing while she waits for you to lead.

Your inner baby takes you back to ego, comparison, competition, male privilege, and whining. Refrain from squalling until you come up with a way forward. Your mood will magically improve when you see how well she responds.

THE POWER OF TWO

When you put aside your instinct to be distant, you discover that the blend of two beings leads to better results than achieved solo.

The best results are, by definition, not predictable. They're found in the depths of the unknown, where the spark of attraction lies. It's the same place that fueled the in-love stage.

Trust yourself and your partner. Going deeper within is the only way out of the typical predicaments. Within is where you will find the needed energy, creativity, and stamina to match the pressure of your woman's needs.

WHAT'S STOPPING YOU?

You have what a woman needs every moment of every day. You don't have to go get it. When your woman's need arises, you have two choices: fulfillment or failure.

There's no escaping this absolute binary. She makes you choose because she can't fulfill her man-needs by herself. Choosing fulfillment leads to happiness, respect, even adoration.

If you fail, then she is in control. If she brings up topics you're afraid of, you get defensive, withdrawn, or angry. Were you in control of your reactions? Nope.

She learns to tip-toe. Then pulls away.

The truth of the relationship is happening all the time, no matter how hard you try to keep it within your comfort zone. That truth rises to the surface at inconvenient times.

Being in love is a peak experience and, therefore, not permanent. Like a months-long MDMA (Ecstasy) trip, when you're high, you're confident, capable, and secure.

Sadly, a high that lasts forever is beyond biological limits. Body systems have to rebound and return to normal operating ranges. The downshift is unwelcome.

You might feel wretched, hungover, or plagued by doubt, but your partner still needs you. Frazzled nerves put you on edge. It helps to have a go-to subroutine.

Failure sequence:
Wretched, think lousy thoughts, blame partner for making you angry, lose control, blow up.

Fulfillment sequence:
Wretched, share, feel better, figure out a strategy, solve a problem, forward movement.

This is the crux. Will you manage yourself into an uplifting connection with your lover? Or get pissy? I know which one feels better.

Some of the best moments with my lover come when I rise from the depths. Fragility seems to enhance my empathetic abilities. That correlation has lowered my fear of fragility to almost nil.

I know I won't have to suffer in silence, keep dark thoughts to myself, and be responsible without reward. I either reveal my sketchy state or, through empathetic action, it vanishes on its own.

Your state is easily observable. Your partner will be relieved to know she is not the cause. But it only works if you're sharing a vulnerability, not a grouchy tongue-lashing.

One can look at this as self-care. If something in your world, like drinking too much coffee, or a critical boss, makes you tense enough to snap at your partner, it's time to work on self-management.

I'm afraid to say that there's no excuse. The feminine isn't protected by invisible shielding. It can't distinguish between ignorant, unintentional, and loss-of-control injuries.

Vulnerable revealing is the type of communication your partner needs. You can initiate it.

Connection is healing to your mind, body, and spirit. Ego-enforcing habits block that path. You may think sharing is a sign of weakness. It's not weak if sharing allows you to release stress, then emerge grounded and centered.

Avoid descending into a bottomless pit of self-pity, however. Self-pity is a journey into the brittleness of ego. Ego reinforcement ultimately backfires. Like trying to stand on top of a basketball, falling off is inevitable.

A calm ego allows connection, empathy, and sexual pleasure, while shielding you from expectations, fear, and shame. The less distracted your internal state, the more you can be present for your lover when her emotions come up.

That means you don't recoil in horror from her emotions, or meet them with the distance of logic. You dive in and give her your presence.

She needs your masculine presence. If you like torture, then don't give her what she needs.

Clinging to your limitations is not masculine. Fear of embarrassment is not masculine. Being overwhelmed by her emotions is not masculine. Fear of your own emotions is not masculine.

Fear of change is not masculine. Fear, generally, is not sexy. And no amount of hiding from your fears makes them go away. Your woman wants you to face them. Work on your fears when she brings them up.

Everything that she wants from you makes you a better man.

I understand. I used to get cranky when my partners wanted to do something I wasn't good at. Even now, I can slip into self-consciousness if Cheryl and I go dancing or to an improv class. It's hard for me to not judge my limited ability.

But melting down helps neither of us. It's a dead end. Dumping my insecure thoughts before I'm too far down the rabbit hole is so much easier.

Whether she is ecstatic or struggling, she wants you to join her. She knows how to live. There is nothing easier than joining her.

THE INTIMACY-RESISTANT MASCULINE

If you're like most men, analytical thinking is a go-to place, particularly under pressure from an intimate partner.

What kind of pressure? Swirling in the flow of life, she wants to catch up, decide, or make a plan, now! But the analytical mind would rather think it over, perhaps indefinitely. It wants to stay in its comfort zone. An effort of will is required to transition from thought to action.

If you object, I'm not speaking about your professional or work behaviors, only what you do when alone with your intimate partner.

She would like some intimacy, meaning a cozy, vulnerable sharing of feelings, states, or processes. But feelings aren't rational. They make no sense. They seem foreign to the analytical mind. Perhaps repugnant.

Of course, women have rational minds and they use them most of the time, but they want their interactions with their lovers to be dominated by transitions from distance to closeness.

The male partner just wants to relax, have a drink, go blank, cruise, watch football, perhaps play a video game. Some form of doing his own thing.

Talking, sharing, planning and negotiating sound exhausting. He wants to put such things off, if possible. And he is frequently successful at this.

The problem is, every time he puts off catching up with his partner, he adds more material to catch up on later. You can do the math.

Slowly, unaddressed material drags on the functioning of a relationship, like a car's oil pan running low on lubrication. Maintenance is required before the motor seizes up.

The urge to ignore signs of distance and isolation eventually feels empty, even to men. We know in our guts that something is off.

A lack of familiarity with emotion causes men to suppress emotional pain instead of delving into the meat of it. They default to the analysis habit, backed up by male-centered reality constructs.

However, the rational mind isn't aware of the underlying emotions that influence its conclusions. It may even resort to gaslighting to overcome objections.

When the intimacy-resistant masculine hides emotions behind rational prognostications, it hurts the feminine enough to make her angry. She feels the disconnect between the suppressed emotions and the rationalization.

She wants to bring her man's panic, fear, and angst to the surface. He usually rebuffs her initiative. Later, she doesn't take it well when his true feelings leak out.

There's nothing wrong with stoic self reliance, when used appropriately. But that's the rub. From a female partner's view, it's overused, denying a large part of what a woman offers.

An intimacy-resistant masculine may escalate into subtle or overt criticism. By finding fault, he shifts the spotlight of pressure back on her.

It seems like nothing to him, but she receives it as contempt, one of the four communication pitfalls that spell doom for a relationship, according to the world-famous Gottman Institute.

A man's discomfort-induced contempt pushes the feminine away. Later, he wonders why she is gone.

RUINING A GOOD THING

Women offer a good thing, but men push it away, every day, many times a day, via subtle messaging. Their body language indicates they're disturbed, annoyed, or disgusted by their partner's attempts to engage and connect.

They want to be left alone in their separateness, so they recoil from their woman's need for intimacy and connection. This habit backfires big time, because her connection needs are fundamental.

She copes as well as she can, but unmet needs push a woman towards a darker place. This all too common progression makes me sad, since I know how easy it is to meet a woman's needs.

I present to you a radical concept: A woman primarily meets her own needs. Her active mind creates fantasies and runs stories that overlay reality and make her man more appealing than he really is.

Men are frightened by the romantic passion of their partners, so try to undermine it. And they're successful. They crush their woman's spirit by dragging her happiness down to earth.

Yet men offer nothing in return. They believe women should get aroused the masculine way, and are miffed when they don't. The genders then settle in for a gradual decline in sexual fire.

Hopefully, you will now see an easy way to meet one of her needs: Don't purposefully dampen her excitement. Specifically, don't recoil from, nitpick, or pop her romance bubble.

Nature made her a romantic. The sane option is to embrace this playful feminine and not cancel the internal Broadway musical that makes her glow. You benefit from her glow of love. Bask in it.

Out of nowhere, she will enthusiastically proclaim, "I love you!"

This is not the time to think deeply and analyze with precision. In less than a second, if there's any amount of love for her in your heart, then reply, "I love you too!"

Any love is love. There is no such thing as forty-three percent love. As a bonus, exclaiming love seeds the feeling of love. What happens if you hesitate and then decide to ignore the topic or side track it?

You lose. Her body will feel rejected. A lover's emotional expressions require you to rise to the occasion. Go in-depth with her and avoid trashing her needs.

FIVE MASCULINE BEHAVIORS

Women are drawn to men who make them feel feminine. A hot bod, hip clothes, a deep voice, and a winning smile can do that, for a while. But at some point, behaviors rise in importance.

The next five sections describe masculine behaviors unique to my area of expertise. They're based on my years of work with women who needed help after shutting down emotionally and sexually.

You can find many other lists of what women find attractive, but this list covers a specific moment: actions to take when feminine needs arise.

And arise they will, as your woman seeks to build upon the lovely image she sees with you. Your physical body, tone of voice, and word choice allow her to enjoy her dreamscape.

Choose the path of her enjoyment. Her mood is malleable. She's open to changing her state, to feel pleasantly massaged instead of tired.

With enough repetitions helping improve her state, she associates you with "yummy good." She doesn't keep a data log of pluses and minuses. She's just magnetically drawn, or not.

The man who helps a woman drop in to her feminine side is a precious resource, since the backdrop of culture and most of the men she interacts with apply pressure for her to be more masculine.

At the end of a day navigating the masculine world, women crave the softness of their feminine nature. They want their men to take over the masculine role.

I learned this while dating escorts, Dakinis, and other sex workers. These women were hot! And knew what worked for them sexually. Sometimes they would tell me about clients that wanted to date them.

That was always accompanied by a sigh and a shake of the head. An escort is happy to cater to a man's needs if she's well paid. But at home, she wants a man who can take over the set and setting of her sex life.

No matter what rung of the social, financial, or economic ladder a woman is on, she is always a woman, and would like to lean on a man every once in a while.

That makes a man the object for her needs. This is not a problem. Men are made for it. The only problem is if men believe a woman should have zero needs. That's when the arrangement falls apart.

A man is fully, deeply, even desperately needed every once in a while. Sadly, at that precise moment, many men decide it's the perfect time to speak about their backlog of slights, imperfections, and criticisms.

Instead of welcoming an opportunity to revel in their inborn masculine, they present their wounded ego. The consequences of such bad timing is almost impossible to recover from.

That is when, maybe for the first time, she takes a step back. Any steps forward after that will be more tentative. It will take time and effort to rebuild trust.

As an introvert, I understand the tendency to stay separate and avoid dealing with issues. What I've found, however, is that underlying tension with my partner interferes with the relaxation I crave.

So, I've learned that initiating connection with her, and processing whatever's up, all the way to the end, is the best way to get back to ease. That takes time, but offers satisfaction and clarity in return.

Never forget that state trumps content. The state of stress is the primary cause of relationship breakups. Successfully managing stress is the next best option after fucking her brains out.

You can be the antidote for the constant pressure from the masculine world to devalue and disregard her feminine essence. Whether she's thrilled and happy, or discouraged and sad, join with her and expand your understanding of life.

ONE: DELIGHT IN THE FEMININE

The very existence of the feminine threatens the masculine by pointing out that it's not complete within itself.

Women make up fifty percent of heterosexual relationships. We can't ignore the math of it. We can't ignore the female voice if we desire relationship success.

Every woman likes the feel of the feminine within her. She wants it to be honored and respected because it's the essence of her being.

Delighting in the feminine is an enjoyable way of honoring it. Get lit by feminine beauty, curves, and softness, but also by words, voice, opinion, activities, and viewpoint.

Delighting means smiling, laughing, complimenting, and joining in with the feminine. When she ascends the stage, put aside your current distraction. Give her your attention. Let her bask in your presence until she's fulfilled.

There's no better option. She must receive the supportive attention she needs, or she will exact retribution. Her punishments are terrible, her rewards magnificent.

The more quickly and thoroughly one ravenously consumes the feminine, which is a joy in itself, the more quickly the feminine feels complete, and can go on to her next thing. She may even leave you hanging, wanting more.

But that's a good thing, right? Wanting more stimulates the dopamine rush of desire. Learn to be quick on your feet. To stand up, to dance, to follow her mood changes, her topic jumping, her interweaving of thoughts, feelings, and sensations.

The feminine is fluid, not logical and step-by-step. But don't worry. When the feminine is flowing, just look on in awe and try to flow with it as much as you can. At the very least, don't recoil from it and try to fight it, like a foreign invader.

Making time and space for the feminine is a gift. It offers a set of new possibilities. A pleasure if you embrace it. A pain if you reject it.

Rejection of the feminine is simply fear. Fear that you're not worthy, might be influenced, or might have to change. Your woman will see your fear. It can't be masked. Fear of your woman is not sexy.

The attractive masculine decisively switches from fear of the feminine to delighting in the feminine. Do it whenever that fear strikes. Don't worry. The feminine is not out to hurt you. It just wants to be itself.

Switch to delight when you have the urge to shrink. You win when she's uplifted. Delight is paid back many times over. And it's so easy. All you have to do is acknowledge her and appreciate her.

She needs positive feedback more than you realize. It feels good to give it. She glows, then associates that glow with you. She'll never stop wanting it. Accept that and make giving appreciation effortless for you.

Join in with her positive states without thinking. Like jumping off a thirty-foot cliff into a deep pool, let her carry you away with her excitement, joy, courage, or sexual arousal. She's offering you the gift of feeling good. Take it.

TWO: MOVE TOWARDS HER

If you delight in the feminine, you move towards it, like a moth to a flame, whatever fuel the flame is burning.

She could be angry about a work problem, excited about an upcoming dance party, or grieving over the death of a pet. Emotions are not a threat, simply an opportunity for the masculine to be masculine.

Emotional expression is not a problem to be fixed. It's the fix itself. Your woman may ask you to fix physical objects, such as a squeaky door hinge, but she doesn't want you to fix her emotions. And she absolutely does *not* want logic or Mansplaining.

The feminine need for emotional expression is so great, it takes precedent over any reaction you might have to the content of her words or style of emoting. Even when the word "you" is in the sentence.

Avoid diversions into logic, invalidation, or defensiveness. These are forms of rejection. It's easy to see that your woman is feeling rejected, if you pause to look at her.

Consciously override rejection tendencies by moving into a comforting position. While it's true that emotional expression is a radiation of energy, it has no mass. It's physically harmless. Don't let it push you away.

Man: "How are you?"
Woman: "It was tense at work today."
Man: "Here we go again."

Hopefully, you got a laugh from that brief script. Of course, it would not be funny to your female partner. Four words just made her day worse, instead of better. Is she drawn to someone who consistently makes her feel worse? No.

She needs to share or process, all the way to the end. In most cases, she'll reach her state of completion with no effort on your part, other than controlling your urge to interdict.

Every two cents you try to insert will cost you many dollars in recovery from her frustration. You become the problem if your reaction interferes with her flow.

Emotional expression is what she needs. Demonstrate that her content and manner of expressing are not a threat by leaning in to closer connection.

THREE: BE AUTHENTIC, BUT NOT HURTFUL

Women like authentic men, bad or good. A bad boy, an alpha, or a rock star can make a woman wet, even without direct contact.

That is nature in action. Women want what makes them feel aroused. If your authentic desire, intensity, passion, artistry, humor, skill set, or even emotional outbursts make your woman wet, then lucky you.

On the flip side, when those things don't make your woman wet, when she's disappointed in you or suggests you could improve, then it feels authentic to defend yourself.

But that is a false authenticity. It feels real because it's habitual, but it primarily covers for a sensitive ego. No defense is needed if you're secure in your self-image.

It may seem like you're simply countering facts with facts, but check yourself for certain indicators. If your ears are hot, your jaw muscles flexed, your cheeks flushed, or you're suddenly self-conscious, you're having an emotional reaction.

Impartiality toward facts is compromised.

Such reactions are normal. It's almost impossible to not have an emotional reaction when your woman illuminates a side of you that doesn't fit your self image. The emotional reaction is what's real.

Real authenticity is acknowledging what underlies the impulse to defend. The urge to be offended and even strike back is about you, not her. It's a stark reveal of weakness.

I contend that anger at one's lover is most accurately seen as self-anger. When a man's capabilities are suddenly diminished from a weakness revealing itself, the shame can be unbearable.

Out of desperation, he may seek to relieve his pain by targeting the witness. But his woman is innocent. He's the one who didn't deal with an issue before it became an emotional sore spot.

Every side-step of an opportunity makes raising the topic harder the next time. Relationship maintenance is a shared responsibility. A man dodges his half if he ignores the blips on his radar.

He may believe he's locked his upsets safely within a mental compartment, but that is a dangerous delusion. His suppressed humiliation, shame, and fear will eventually degrade his attraction her.

A man's authenticity is tainted by legacy, a backlog of hurts, and a lack of emotional maturity. He must be doubly and triply self-aware when the impulse to defend or attack arises.

The source of the impulse could be a childhood scolding, a date rejection, or a conflict with a former partner. However, it will feel like one's current partner is the source.

This is why it's important to clarify the purity of authentic-seeming impulses. One may have to analyze the impulse several times to get it right, just like reworking a questionable text.

The effort to clarify is not a sacrifice. It saves the Herculean task of making up for hurtful expressions that stubbornly resist healing.

Just being themselves, women sometimes injure a man's ego. That's when the moment of humiliation, shame, or fear hits. In an instant, he's gut-punched.

The urge to trade a hurt for a hurt rises up. She senses a wave of contempt and backs away. She would much rather her man confess to being hurt. Vulnerability is the true sign of strength and confidence.

Vulnerability means not being afraid of one's weaknesses and imperfections, at least to a love mate. I can't say this enough: The urge to defend and attack is a sign of weakness, not strength.

It's not fair, but female partners look to their men for steadiness under pressure. To handle what is, instead of breaking down. This dynamic forces men into more maturity than they might prefer.

Obviously, women get triggered too. However, they are more likely to reveal their wounding, instead of covering it with a hurtful rebuke. They deserve a smidgeon of slack for this.

Women are also more receptive to opening up and making progress on issues. In this manner, they make halting progress.

Men are susceptible to resentment towards women's abilities to process emotions and advance in skills. That resentment lies dormant, waiting for the moment a woman becomes vulnerable and in need of support to launch an attack.

Her sharing of an authentic need highlights his inability to do the same. The imbalance feels unfair. Perhaps he wants her to magically fix him, instead of having to delve into his issues.

A habit of keeping difficulties, needs, imbalances, and weaknesses to oneself erects a wall between lovers. To a woman, this feels like her man has pulled away. She instinctively does the same.

Being in relationship puts pressure on a man to face his demons. That is never fun, but there's no option to healing one's defensive over-reactions.

However, the rewards are priceless. When a healthy masculine comes forth, inborn abilities, unknown strengths, and perhaps a playful bad boy breaks out.

All of those are turn ons.

FOUR: FUNCTIONAL UNDER PRESSURE

Stress is the biggest factor disturbing relationship peace. The stress of fulfilling the "man role" is a major contributor. Men receive training within their professions to manage employees, meet goals, and increase productivity.

But when do they learn to be the man in a relationship? Some part of that comes naturally, but never the whole package, so stress related to one's intimate partner is inevitable.

When the stressor arises, a functional response is the most productive. Notice when you are collapsing, shutting down, and becoming defeated by something going on with your partner, or something the two of you are equally stressed about.

It will take practice to recognize the exact moment a stressor takes over, because it happens so fast. Acceptance is a useful next step. It's too late to complain or argue. The stressor has already taken control.

Stress reactions are not the problem. They're a normal part of living. Welcome them as a stimulating input that gives energy for taking action.

The actual problem is the situation causing the stress reaction. Dealing with that situation is the relief from stress, so the sooner one takes action, the more easily a pit of despair is avoided.

The pressure is on. Your woman is watching to see what you will do. This is the point at which legacy insecurities verge on flare up. They can't be allowed to smother functionality. Interventions are handy.

You could sigh, breathe deeply, yawn, groan, cry, or laugh uproariously. Release a little tension, then search within for something that could help manage the stressful situation.

The challenge increases in difficulty when the source of stress is content your woman has communicated. She may have revealed that you don't meet a need of hers, or you've broken an agreement and she's disappointed.

Taut situations need to be managed as they arise. There's no going back to a time before. The current moment is won or lost, forever.

Guide yourself away from the urge to collapse or lash out. Categorize discomfort as purely physical. *My bowels just turned to water. My knees just got weak. I suddenly became dizzy.*

Like an autoimmune disorder, your body overreacts to mental viruses by attacking itself. The sensations of illness are serious, but temporary. You will survive, and improve, if you use stress for motivation.

Relationship stress is merely an indicator that a glitch needs fixing. Partners offer a gift when they reveal the glitch, since it is then out in the open and can be addressed.

Jump on it instead of fighting against it. No matter what the content is, if it's disturbing then it highlights a weakness. Your reaction to your uncovered weaknesses is on you.

A woman seeing your weaknesses is nothing. She sees them all the time. Doing nothing about your weaknesses is a *real* problem.

The game is *How do I make progress on my weaknesses, real time, under pressure, in full view of my woman?* The answer, or result, is a clear test of how you handle yourself.

Handling yourself is waiting until the best of you dominates the worst of you. That is truly what she needs and all you ever have to provide. The best of you.

She puts pressure on you to be your best. I used to hate that pressure. The thought of having to up-level, improve, or do better made my nerves hurt, as if I were running a mile on a sprained ankle.

But that pain went away when I stopped resenting my lover's needs. Now, if I notice myself dipping into self-pity (about the pressure my woman is putting on me), I know how to address it. I immediately seek to meet her needs.

Poof! Pain gone.

For sure, you need a platform for self-pity. Your woman can help you with topics not directly related to her. Otherwise, use a coach or therapist.

Self-pity, complaining, and whining are ways to vent emotional overwhelm. There's no shame in admitting the need for it, then sourcing someone who can hear it. Vent to the sky and trees, in a pinch.

Venting is separate from the rational discussion of your wants, needs, and boundaries. The more you vent, the more you will understand your actual needs, instead of the squalling baby inside you.

Whatever is bugging you is affecting everything. The sooner you deal with it, the sooner it ceases to drag you down. Initiate a discussion, negotiation, vulnerable sharing, or comforting hug.

After countless cycles of putting off care-taking my vulnerable authentic self until my revengeful side attacked my partner, I got sick of making messes and learned a new way.

A go-to technique I use to reverse the symptoms of pressure distress is to laser-focus on aspects of my woman that I unfailingly like, such as her boobs, her smell, her smile, her touch.

Create your own list. After a few minutes of pleasurable distraction, you may regain enough functionality to courageously and creatively lead yourself and your partner to a win for you both.

FIVE: OWN YOUR SHIT

No matter how skilled you are in every aspect of life, no matter how alpha or buff or rich you are, you have an Achilles Heel.

Any time you feel queasy or uncertain about your partner's loyalty, sexual satisfaction, or opinion of you, your Achilles Heel has pinged. It's an alert that chimes under specific circumstances while you're interacting with your partner.

Queasiness is caused by an adrenaline dump into the stomach. The body does this to prepare for threats. In this case, the threat is a partner-induced ego challenge.

Adrenaline urges a quick response. To go with the first instinct, such as denial, invalidation, or anger. Access to thoughtful introspection is blocked off.

Clear thinking takes a back seat to partner-directed and self-directed negative exaggerations. As the mental mines explode, functionality tanks. The effects range in severity, but the problem is shit, to put it crudely.

Shit is our unprocessed wounding suffered in the presence of a woman. No man escapes life without some woman's rejection, judgment, criticism, or abuse.

The miseries linger and perhaps never completely heal. One survival tactic is to suppress flashes of previous trauma, inadequacy, and lack of skills, by pretending nothing is wrong.

But some aspect of a man's behavior will give the game away and his woman will wonder what's going on. She may apply pressure to find out.

Assume you're hiding some shit that messes things up with your lady. It would be nice to fix that, right? Start by owning it. Acknowledge to yourself the tiniest thought or feeling related to your partner that threatens to crash you.

No amount of denial helps. There's no escape from working on your shit before the pain in your guts overrides the pleasure in your cock. A woman wants your unbridled passion.

If your shit gets in the way of your passion, you deny her what she needs. She may proclaim her love and commitment, but her body is the decider. It knows when something is amiss. It stops getting turned on.

She may not realize what's wrong, but the effect is the same. She is drawn in, or pushed away, by an invisible director buried deep within her man's head.

He may feel love and enthusiasm, at times, but the pain of self-consciousness neutralizes the fleeting pleasures of oneness. At important moments, such as making love, worry about his performance overrides every other feature.

He can't win. If she derives pleasure, he is envious. If she doesn't, he feels guilty. There's no end to stresses that stab the ego. The pain is correlated with her, but she is not the cause.

The cause is a primal emotion, such as shame, that pushes a man to reject his partner. He rejects the feminine for wanting a satisfying love life, since his limitations make that impossible for him.

His signs of rejection may not be obvious, but as pressure continues, tendencies towards jealousy, misogyny, or pettiness emerge.

You may see the problem. A man's internal pain gets inflicted on his partner. Pain his partner doesn't deserve. Women are all too familiar with the downside of men's unprocessed issues.

They know from experience that buried emotional mines are difficult to access and defuse. Even unexploded, they affect everything that happens in the relationship, like a troublesome housemate.

This is the angst of so many women. Should I stay or go? It would be convenient if their bodies got turned on and had orgasms, regardless of the minefield. There might be an incentive to stay. Alas, that's not how it works.

Nature made her desire a man. He was encouraging at first, but later rejects her. When she gets the hint and pulls away, the man whines about it.

She would like to make it work. Walking away is a big deal. She made an emotional investment. She doesn't want to take the loss and have to start over.

But she won't accept ongoing hopelessness. There's a window of opportunity, when a man decides that his Achilles Heel will not destroy a good thing. That's a demonstration of character a woman is drawn to.

If you collapse in the face of a woman's need for your best, you're not confident in yourself. There's no in-between. A man is confident, or not, and women expertly detect the difference.

In order to appear confident and uncollapsed, a man may dissociate from his internal turmoil. But his woman notices his lack of presence.

Her attempts to bring the interaction back into connection are usually unsuccessful. The man has practice steering away from touchy subjects. His misdirection, or gaslighting, invalidates her intuition. Both partners lose.

The truth, acknowledged or not, controls the relationship dynamic. Imagine that your woman seemed less enthusiastic than usual during the latest sexual get-together. You wonder if you should say something. You're curious, but also anxious.

After a demure hesitation, your woman reveals that your fingernails scratched her vagina. It was a minor irritation, but it distracted her from reaching a peak of pleasure.

After the shock of unpleasant surprise, how would you respond? Would you fall into a rabbit hole of self pity? Would you agonize over how women make everything difficult?

Or would you be indignant? Would you deny that your nails are under-groomed? Would you proclaim that she's too sensitive, then get mad if she objects?

Hopefully, you can see that both responses would be terrible. What if you didn't take the comment as another wound to your ego and offered to be more diligent filing your nails?

There will always be something to tweak, in order to continue the best functioning of both partners. Odds are, a woman's input is an attempt to improve something, not take you down.

Regardless of partner's feedback, your impulse to freeze, fight, or flee indicates you're responding emotionally. Like a baby Alien, the sensations of emotion are thrashing around under your skin.

If you can't identify which emotion, use fear. Example fear: *She's giving me a sexy vibe right now, but I'm tired and might have trouble getting an erection.*

Is her interest in sex the problem? No, the scary thought is the problem. Dump the thought, or turn it into sexual action, before her enthusiasm dissipates.

You are the only source of debilitating emotions. Yes, there is a correlation between your partner and your fear. But correlation is not causation.

A correlation is when two things happen in a close time sequence. You take a drink of water, then cough. Did the water make you cough? No. Not swallowing properly made you cough. The cause was a glitch in your throat.

It's vitally important to deal with glitches, which are primarily triggers, when they come up, so they don't steadily get worse. Thankfully, your woman gives you many opportunities to do that.

ARE YOU ON BOARD?

Men have been fleeing in terror of the feminine for millennia. Masculine ideals of the past omitted any hint of the feminine and both sexes have suffered ever since.

It's time for that to change. Love, sex, and connection are the currency of the feminine, but both genders have that need.

Denial of human needs results in dysfunction. I'm frequently called upon to help repair the damage. That takes more work than anyone realizes.

Damage *prevention* is far easier. If you're on board, it may be counterproductive to speak about it to your lover, partner, or spouse. The proof will be in the pudding.

It's difficult to change habits. You will mess up. The learning curve is steep.

When you mess up, apologize (for rebuffing or not fulfilling her need) and try again.

Don't expect your woman to help you with this. She just wants you to do it.

She may not respond as much as you hope, initially. It may take some time for her to feel safe with you again.

Trust is built through actions. Promises are worthless, but there is always an action you can take.

Try out the five masculine behaviors today and gradually soak up the lessons in this book. It's hard to overstate how much better your relationship can be.

Email me with questions about concepts, or to share results.

You can help spread the message of successful male-female communication by posting a book review.

Seva Kenn

seva@makeloveeasy.coach
makeloveeasy.coach/seva

BIBLIOGRAPHY

Adams, H and Et al. "Is Homophobia Associated with Homosexual Arousal? - PubMed." PubMed, pubmed.gov, 1996, https://pubmed.ncbi.nlm.nih.gov/8772014/.

Bergner, Daniel. *What Do Women Want?: Adventures in the Science of Female Desire.* Ecco, An Imprint of HarperCollins Publishers, 2014.

Barling, Julian. The Science of Leadership: Lessons from Research for Organizational Leaders. Oxford University Press, 2014.

Barling, Julian. The Science of Leadership. Oxford University Press, 2014.

Birdwhistell, Ray. "How Much of Communication Is Really Nonverbal? - PGi Blog." PGi Blog, https://www.facebook.com/PgiFans/, 30 Mar. 2020, https://www.pgi.com/blog/2020/03/how-much-of-communication-is-really-nonverbal/.

Duncan, Joe. "New Studies Confirm People Care Less About Looks Than They Used To." The Science of Sex | Joe Duncan | Substack, The Science of Sex, 27 Mar. 2022, https://the-scienceofsex.substack.com/p/new-studies-confirm-people-care-less?

Folkman, Joseph and Jack Zenger. The Ideal Praise-to-Criticism Ratio. *Harvard Business Review*, 27 June 2017, hbr.org/2013/03/the-ideal-praise-to-criticism.

Gillihan, Seth J. Why Do Couples Fight-and How Can They Stop. *Psychology Today*, Sussex Publishers, 21 Feb. 2018, www.psychologytoday.com/us/blog/think-act-be/201802/why-do-couples-fight-and-how-can-they-stop.

Helm, Fonya. "WHAT DESTROYS LOVE? - Fonya Lord Helm PhD, ABPP - Clinical Psychologist - Psychoanalyst." *https://www.facebook.com/fonya.helm?fref=ts*, 19 May 2015, https://fonyahelm.com/what-destroys-love/.

Huberman, Andrew. Tools for Managing Stress & Anxiety | Huberman Lab Podcast #10. YouTube, 8 Mar. 2021, https://www.youtube.com/watch?v=ntfcfJ28eiU.

Keltner, Dacher. "Hands On Research: The Science of Touch." Greater Good, Greater Good Magazine, 29 Sept. 2010, *https:// greatergood.berkeley.edu/article/item/ hands_*on_research.

Nishizawa, S., and Et al. "Differences between Males and Females in Rates of Serotonin Synthesis in Human Brain." PubMed Central (PMC), Proc Natl Acad Sci U S A, 13 May 1997, https://www.ncbi.nlm.nih.gov/pmc/articles/ PMC24674/.

Santos-Longhurst, Adrienne. "High Cortisol Symptoms: What Do They Mean?" Healthline, Healthline Media, 31 Aug. 2018, https:// www.healthline.com/health/high-cortisol-symptoms.

Volker, Et al. "Effect of Deep and Slow Breathing on Pain Perception, Autonomic Activity, and Mood Processing—An Experimental Study | Pain Medicine | Oxford Academic." OUP Academic, Oxford University Press, 23 Feb. 2012, https://academic.oup.com/ painmedicine/article/13/2/215/1936333.

Made in the USA
Middletown, DE
02 December 2022

16169858R00049